MARTIAL ARTS

TAE KWON DO

David Amerland

Raintree

Contents

Introduction

Nothing illustrates the ability of the human body to exceed its own limitations better than martial arts, and tae kwon do is the most spectacular of all martial arts. A cross between high-kicking, spinning jump kicks and gymnastics, tae kwon do can be a key to unlock the full potential of your body and mind. What's more, it's a martial art which can become exactly what you are willing to make of it.

History

The Korean flag with yin & yang and I-Ching symbols.

Tae kwon do is over 2000 years old. Like most forms of unarmed combat, it developed out of necessity in its homeland, Korea, in about 57 BC.

This mural from the Koguryo period (about AD 400), at the Anak Tomb, North Korea, depicts two warriors engaged in taek kyon *fighting.*

Originally known as *taek kyon*, it was used as a means of defence against wild animals but was soon incorporated in the military training of the emperor's young soldiers. At the time, Korea was divided into three separate kingdoms, and they were often at war with each other. After almost half a millennium of friction, one of these kingdoms – the Silla kingdom – won. Many of its soldiers were members of an elite group of young men called *hwa rang do* who practised *taek kyon*, and were devoted to cultivating their minds and bodies to the highest level possible. They developed an honour code which today forms the basis of tae kwon do.

Tae kwon do is best known in martial arts for its spectacularly fast, accurate kicks.

Tenets of tae kwon do

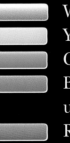 The philosophy of tae kwon do is based upon constant striving for excellence. The goal is to become an honourable person with perfect character and fitness.

The martial arts skills learned in tae kwon do are used to prevent conflict and violence, not to initiate it.

COURTESY – Courtesy to all those around us is a core principle in tae kwon do. Students must show respect to their instructors, to higher ranking students and to all others.

INTEGRITY – One must be able to define right and wrong and have the conscience, if wrong, to feel remorse.

PERSEVERANCE – Nothing of any lasting value comes easily. If you fail the first time, or even the hundredth time, try again.

SELF CONTROL – This tenet is extremely important inside and outside the *dojang* (school or gymnasium).

INDOMITABLE SPIRIT – Never be afraid to be yourself and trust your judgement. Keep your ideals and your identity.

BELTS
The philosophy of tae kwon do is expressed in the belt colour system.

WHITE signifies innocence.
YELLOW signifies Earth.
GREEN signifies growth.
BLUE signifies heaven and upwards development.
RED signifies danger, caution, control.
BLACK signifies closure and the maturity of the student.

1

2

3

4

HOW TO TIE A BELT
1 Hold belt so that two thirds of it are on your right-hand side.
2 Wrap it around your body twice, making sure that each loop falls on itself.
3 Bring the right-hand side belt behind both loops and make a knot in a left-over-right fashion.
4 Repeat left-over-right with the two ends.

Clothing & equipment

ITF and WTF are the two main styles of tae kwon do. ITF emphasizes a light contact system which encourages fast moves and multiple combinations. WTF promotes power – kicks are straightforward and effective.

Basic clothing is similar in both styles of tae kwon do. White suits are worn by all students and white suits with a black trim are worn by black belts.

In the International Tae Kwon Do Federation (ITF) style, there is no chest protection, but competitors wear groin, mouth and head guards, as well as hand and feet pads. The point scoring system rewards speed and good strategy, not sheer kicking power.

ITF
1 head guard
2 gum shield
3 hand guard
4 groin guard
5 foot guard

In the World Tae Kwon Do Federation (WTF) style of fighting, competitors are expected to wear a head guard, chest protector, groin and mouth guards. The chest protector allows WTF competitors to use stronger kicks.

Because of their fast, powerful kicks, both styles of tae kwon do require competitors to wear an external or under-the-suit groin guard to protect against any mistimed or badly-aimed kicks which could cause serious injury.

WARMING UP

In order to perform high kicks effectively and safely, a great deal of time is given to warming up properly. Stretching exercises are usually performed with the help of a partner, and focus on the hamstrings (tendons on the inside of the thigh) and the hip joint. Stretching partners need to communicate so that they push, but do not exceed each other's stretching limits.

WTF

1 head guard
2 gum shield
3 chest protector
4 groin guard

Forefist punch
(chirugi)

There are two basic straight-line punches thrown in tae kwon do – obverse (the hand punching is on the same side as the lead leg) and reverse (the hand punching is on the opposite side from the lead leg).

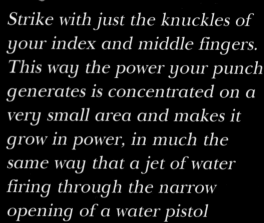

Strike with just the knuckles of your index and middle fingers. This way the power your punch generates is concentrated on a very small area and makes it grow in power, in much the same way that a jet of water firing through the narrow opening of a water pistol becomes a lot more powerful.

OBVERSE PUNCH

Notice the positioning of the feet. They're wide apart, with the lead leg bent slightly and the body weight divided evenly over both feet. This is important, as the power of a punch in tae kwon do is generated by the twisting of the hips as you are about to hit a target. If your feet are not in that position, you can't twist and generate any power.

REVERSE PUNCH

By using the arm opposite the lead leg to punch, the reverse punch permits the upper body to twist faster and further, and generate more power as a result. As in the obverse punch, the feet are about shoulder-width apart, toes pointing forward and the opposite hand is drawn quickly to the waist.

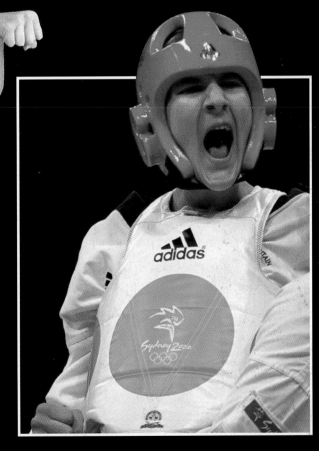

The twisting motion of the hip increases the power of the punch, far beyond what the arm muscles alone could generate.

The kiai, or power cry, starts deep from within your lungs and allows you to focus your mental, emotional and physical energy into a single, devastating strike.

Backfist punch
(dung joomuk)

The backfist is one of the most fluid, powerful and effective punches in tae kwon do. The best way to think of it is as a backhanded slap with a closed fist. It only reaches its full power when the arm is fully extended.

The striking area should be the knuckles of your index and middle fingers.

Cross your wrists at eye-level, backs of the hands towards you. Keep your striking arm on the outside, elbow pointing at the target.

Move both hands at the same time. The inside hand is rapidly returned to the waist, palm facing upwards. The outside hand is pushed out to strike.

REVERSE BACKFIST
The basic backfist can be improved with a little twist.

Face your opponent as you would in the opening stage of any other attacking move. Keep your arms up and body weight on your back leg.

The backfist as a competition technique is lightning fast. As this picture shows, it allows you to extend your shoulder fully, in order to reach an opponent who believes he is safely out of reach.

Begin turning your body in a 360 degree circle, using your front leg as a pivot.

As you line up with your opponent again, cross your wrists as you would for a normal backfist.

Now follow through and strike the target. The blow will have been augmented by the spinning of your body.

Knifehand strike
(sonkal taerigi)

This is the so-called 'karate chop'. It is primarily used against soft tissue targets such as the side of the neck and the throat, but with special training over time, martial artists can toughen their hands to break wooden boards and bricks.

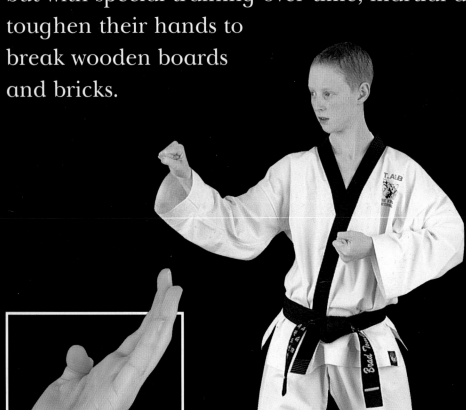

The striking area of the 'karate chop' is the outside edge of the palm. This area has relatively few nerves, and when the hand moves quickly, it can generate considerable power.

Start with the weight of the body distributed mostly on the back leg, with arms held up for protection.

Cross your wrists in front of your face. The striking hand is on the inside, and your protecting arm is on the outside.

KNIFEHAND STRIKE IN COMBAT

Because of their speed and accuracy, knifehand strikes in combat can be aimed at 'difficult' targets such as the base of the neck.

1 Timing is vital when aiming a knifehand strike against a moving opponent.

2 To maximize the impact, you should strike at the moment of an opponent's attack.

...tecting arm travels to your waist, ...wards. The striking arm travels to ...t with the edge of the palm towards ...umb is tucked in to avoid injury.

A knifehand strike is very similar to a knifehand block, used to deflect a kick while keeping the rest of the body out of reach.

Front snap kick
(ap chagi)

The leg is stronger and longer than the arm, and tae kwon do kicks allow a weaker defender to turn the tables on a stronger, physically bigger opponent, and easily defeat him or her.

The ball of the foot should make contact with the target. The toes are carefully bent back to avoid injury. As with punches, the power of the kick is increased by focusing the pressure on a small area.

Spectacular competition kicks demonstrate the grace and awesome power of tae kwon do.

Start with your hands i a guard position, body weight distributed mostly on the back leg and facing the directio of attack.

The front snap kick is a very fast, powerful kick which can also be used in jumping kicks against very high targets.

Shift the body weight entirely on to the back leg and bring your kicking leg into the chamber position (off the ground, bent at a right angle), with the knee pointing at the target you're kicking.

Complete the kick by extending the foot in a straight line to connect with the target. Be careful to bend the toes back to avoid injury and use the ball of the foot to strike.

Turning kick
(dollyo chagi)

A favourite of competition fighters, the turning kick is executed by bringing the foot up, knee bent, then quickly whipping the foot round to make contact with the intended target.

1 Stand with your arms in guard, body weight mostly on the back leg.
2 Shift your body weight entirely to the back leg. Bring your front leg to the chamber position with the knee in
3 Extend your leg to strike the target. The striking area can be the top of your foot (instep) or the ball of your foot. In the latter case, pull your toes back to avoid injury.

1

2

3

FRONT VIEW

18

1

The turning kick is a favourite in both WTF and ITF. It is fast, impressive and easy for scoring umpires to see. It is also useful for self-defence against a careless attacker.

2

3

PRACTICE

The power and accuracy of the turning kick are best practised against a pad with a partner. That way you can get a feel for its effectiveness and practise the kick at different heights, in a controlled manner.

When executed in competition, the kick looks spectacular, and almost never fails to score.

Side kick
(yop chagi)

This is a kick with serious stopping power. Even when used in a semi-contact situation, it has the ability to stop attackers in their tracks.

This kick is risky – when it fails to work, it takes a long time to recover balance and poise, because so much of the body is used. In competition, this can make the difference between a win or a loss.

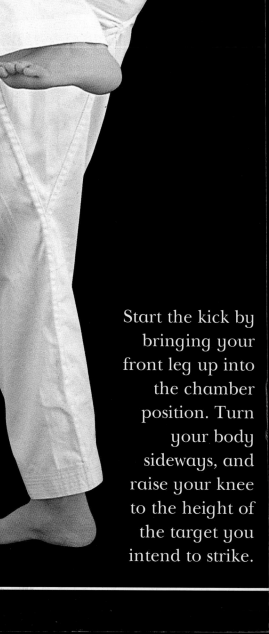

Start the kick by bringing your front leg up into the chamber position. Turn your body sideways, and raise your knee to the height of the target you intend to strike.

The side kick can be aimed at any height. Its power and versatility are seen here in a tae kwon do demonstration.

Extend your leg with the outer edge of the foot towards the target. This is the part of the foot that makes contact during the kick. So, the side kick is the equivalent of a 'karate chop' with the foot.

Nothing matches the speed and stopping power of a correctly executed side kick.

Hook kick
(golcho chagi)

The hook kick is used mostly by ITF competition fighters. This is a fast, arcing kick, designed to strike the side of the head with the back of the heel.

Speed, good balance and flexibility are critical in the correct execution of any kick, particularly when this move is used in the fluid situation of a tae kwon do competition bout.

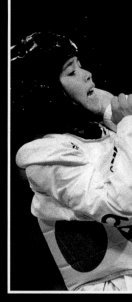

The execution of this kick begins just like all the others by cocking the leg in the chamber position.

At execution, the supporting foot turns to face away from the target, allowing the hip joint greater movement.

TRAINING

A hand-held pad is the perfect target for practising the speed and accuracy of the hook kick. A controlled execution trains specific muscle groups, and helps develop the flexibility and balance you need in kicks aimed at high targets.

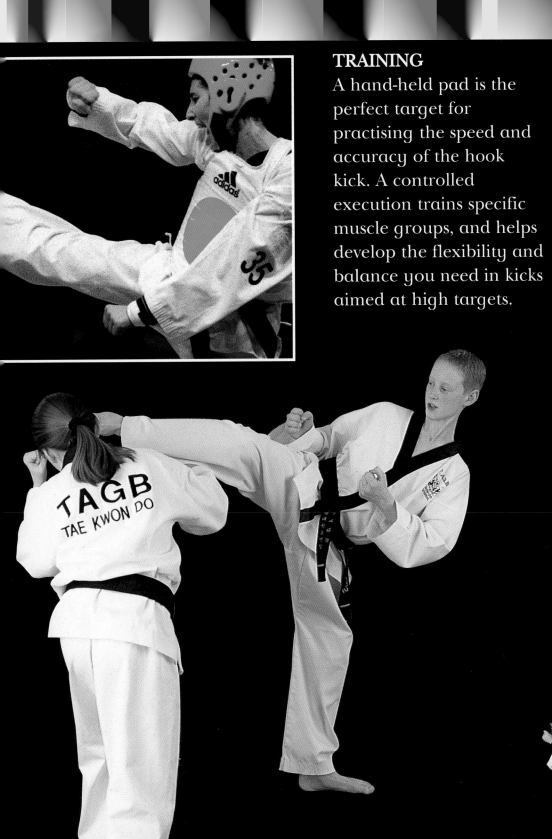

This in turn increases the speed and power with which the kicking leg can be whipped past the target, and gives greater control in the execution of the kick.

Back kick
(dwit chagi)

1   2

A back kick can be used to check an opponent, as well as strike her down.

The back kick is known as a 'stopping kick'. That's because it will stop just about anything you hit with it. Because of the power it generates, it's probably one of the hardest kicks to control. It's best used when breaking objects and in competitions.

The back kick is the human equivalent of a donkey kick.

ITF REVERSE SIDE KICK
The reverse side kick allows the body to spin 180 degrees and use the back leg to kick.

1 Stand in guard position with the body's weight mostly on the back leg. **2** Shift the weight of the body to the front leg and spin on the spot in an anticlockwise direction until the back leg comes to the front. **3** Cock this leg, ready for a side kick. **4** Extend the leg, leading the edge of the foot outward, to strike the intended target.

WTF BACK KICK

1 Stand in a guard position with your weight mostly on the back leg. **2** Turn your lead foot to face behind you and half spin so your back is to the target. **3** Raise your leg, ready to kick straight back. **4** Extend the leg, connecting with the target. Point your toes towards the floor so that the heel of the foot makes contact with the target.

Jumping kick *(twimyo chagi)*

Jumping kicks allow you to strike targets higher and with greater power than would be possible with muscle power alone. They use accuracy, speed and flexibility and are among the most spectacular and effective in the world of martial arts.

JUMPING REVERSE HOOK KICK

1 Start with your hands at guard and body weight evenly distributed on your legs.

2 Bend your knees and take off, spinning the body 180 degrees in an anticlockwise direction.

3-4 As your back leg comes to the front, cock it into the chamber position.

5 Extend the leg to strike through the target as you land.

JUMPING BACK KICK
This is the perfect stopping kick for short-range matches.

1 With your weight evenly distributed on both legs, jump and spin to face away from the opponent.

2 Kick straight back before you land, making contact with your heel.

JUMPING REVERSE SIDE KICK

This kick allows you to make better use of space, to reach a difficult target and generate greater power. Equally useful in competition, sparring, breaking objects and demonstrations, it lets a small opponent fight a bigger and stronger one on almost equal terms.

1 Stand with the feet about shoulder-width apart.
2 Turn your body so that the front leg is now your back one.

3 Jump using both feet, and cock your lead leg in the chamber position. **4** Extend your leg and kick before you land.

Sparring
(*matsoki*)

Free sparring allows you to simulate unarmed combat, and practise the free-flowing kicks and punches you've learnt. Sparring requires strict supervision and safety equipment.

FREE SPARRING
Blue and Red square up against each other.

They change positions, looking for a suitable opening to attack.

SPARRING BOUT

Blue and Red square up at close quarters.

Blue bounces off Red and attacks with a snap kick.

Red anticipates this and counters with a turning kick.

Blue sees Red initiate a turning kick attack.

Blue spins and counters with a reverse side kick.

Blue and Red return to close quarters sparring.

Blue takes a step back, looking for an opening.

Red spots this and uses a back kick to win!

Useful information

Tae kwon do on the web is every bit as intense as tae kwon do in the *dojang*.

TAE KWON DO ASSOCIATION OF
GREAT BRITAIN (TAGB)
www.tagb.biz

TAGB TIMES MAGAZINE
www.tagbtimes.com

UNITED KINGDOM TAE KWON DO
ASSOCIATION (UKTA)
www.ukta.com

WORLD TAE KWON DO FEDERATION
(WTF)
www.wtf.org

TAE KWON DO AUSTRALIA INC.
www.taekwondoaustralia.org.au

All the Internet addresses (URLs) given in this book
were valid at the time of going to press. However, due
to the dynamic nature of the Internet, some addresses
may have changed, or sites may have ceased to exist
since publication. While the author and publishers
regret any inconvenience this may cause readers, no
responsibility for any such changes can be accepted
by either the author or the publishers.

TAE KWON DO ASSOCIATION OF
GREAT BRITAIN
163a Church Road,
Redfield,
Bristol,
BS5 9LA

TAGB TIMES MAGAZINE
TT Centre,
PO Box 90,
Bramhall,
Cheshire,
SK7 2YJ

TAE KWON DO INTERNATIONAL
(TKDI)
5 Tollgate Road,
Southam,
Warwickshire,
CV47 1EE

Tae kwon do terms

ap cha busugi front kick
ap chagi front snap kick
ap cha milgi front pushing kick
bakuro outward moving
bandae dollyo chagi reverse
  turning kick
bandae dollyo goro chagi
  reverse hook kick
bandal chagi crescent kick
bituro chagi twisting kick
cha mom chagi checking kick
chirugi forefist punch
dojang school or gymnasium
dollyo chagi turning kick
dung joomuk backfist
duro scooping
dwijibo upset
dwit bal rear foot
dwit chagi back kick
dwitja jurigi back piercing kick
golcho hooking
golcho chagi hook kick
goro chagi sweeping kick
guburyo bending
gunnun walking
gyoroogi sparring
ibo matsoki two-step sparring

ilbo matsoki one-step sparring
japp yosul tae release from grab
jayoo matsoki free sparring
junbi ready
makgi block
miro pushing
nachuo low
naeryo chagi downward kick
nakka chagi hook kick
narani parallel
noolo pressing
olligi rising kick
ollyo upward
palmok daebi forearm guarding
sambo matsoki three-step
  sparring
sang palmok twin forearm
sang sonkal twin knife hand
so bandae reverse
so baro obverse
sogarak joomuk knuckle fist
sonkal daebi knifehand
  guarding
sonnal chigi knifehand strike
waebal one leg
yop side
yop chagi side kick

Index